T0055966

WILLIAM MATHIAS

PROCESSIONAL

MUSIC DEPARTMENT

OXFORD
UNIVERSITY PRESS

PROCESSIONAL

WILLIAM MATHIAS

© Oxford University Press 1965

Printed in Great Britain

OXFORD UNIVERSITY PRESS, MUSIC DEPARTMENT, GREAT CLARENDON STREET, OXFORD OX2 6DP

The Moral Rights of the Composer have been asserted. Photocopying this copyright material is ILLEGAL.

Sw.
mp
Gt.
mf
(Sw.)
Gt.
mf
f
Sw.
Sw.
p
p

mp
p
pp
p
p
Gt.
Gt.
cresc.

Gt. mf
Sw. mp
mf
mp
Sw. mp
Gt.
mf
Gt.
cresc.

allargando
f
a tempo
f
Gt. to Ped.
f
cresc.
ff